WHEAT BELLY SLOW COOKER

30 Delicious Grain-Free Slow Cooker Recipes for Beginners

D1418012

INTRODUCTION

I want to thank you and congratulate you for downloading the book, *"Wheat Belly Slow Cooker: 30 Delicious Grain-Free Slow Cooker Recipes for Beginners"*.

This book contains proven steps and strategies on how to prepare delicious and simple wheat belly diet recipes with a slow cooker.

If you're looking for simple recipes that taste great and take almost no time to prepare, then this is the book for you! The 30 recipes within this book are made with beginning chefs in mind, and are written in easy language with step by step directions. You'll be making wheat belly approved meals in your slow cooker in no time with the help of this book!

Thanks again for downloading this book, I hope you enjoy it!

Table of Contents

Chapter 1 - Wheat Belly

The wheat belly diet was created by Dr. William Davis, a cardiologist who found that every time he ate wheat or products containing wheat, he was bloated and feeling miserable for hours after the fact. He decided that the best way to help himself lose weight would be to cut out wheat and by-products of wheat from his diet, and the results were phenomenal! Now his diet plan is taking the country by storm, and you, too, have the opportunity to lose weight by following a simple wheat belly diet.

Dr. Davis has conducted studies and tests on several patients, himself included, to determine whether or not removing wheat from the diet is really beneficiary to weight loss. He found that the weight loss in his wheat belly patients (and in himself) was astounding. However, weight loss wasn't the only benefit he and the other test patients discovered when they tried out the wheat belly diet. They also found that they had increased levels of energy and mental focus throughout their daily routines. They were able to get more done every day, and didn't even need as much sleep at night as they used to!

The wheat belly diet works because it reduces the intake of carbohydrates on a daily basis. Other diet plans and fads have proven in the past that reducing carbohydrate consumption is one of the best possible ways to initiate weight loss and keep that weight off, too. Because reducing carbohydrates forces the body to use up fat stores for energy, fat is burned extra quickly on low-carb diets.

While the wheat belly diet is low carb, it is not specifically a low carb diet. You can eat carbs that do not come from wheat and wheat products on this diet. However, you must always stay away from grain.   This makes the wheat belly diet very similar to a gluten-free diet, but again, you are allowed to eat gluten when it does not come from wheat or wheat products. In both situations, it would be very simple to adapt the wheat belly diet to include a low-carb and/or gluten-free style of eating, as well.

When following a wheat belly diet, be sure to eat the simplest forms of food you can.   Raw fruits and vegetables can be cooked at home to ensure that you are getting all of their nutrients without purchasing pre-cooked bags of them at the grocery store.   The same is true of meat.   Whenever possible, purchase raw meat and prepare it yourself.   You'll be so glad you did!

On the wheat belly diet, you can eat vegetables, berries, fruit, nuts, seeds, plant-based oils, meat and eggs, cheese, yogurt, butter, soy, olives, avocados, pickled vegetables, and wine. However, you should never eat bread, pasta, cereal, pretzels, barley, rye, spelt, oats, or alcohol such as beer that has been brewed from wheat.   Avoid eating prepackaged and processed foods whenever possible.   In this way, it is also very easy to adopt a paleo lifestyle when you are eating grain-free wheat belly approved foods!   Remember, wheat can show up in foods you would never expect to contain grain, and it is of course one of the main ingredients in things like breakfast cereals, bagels, fried foods, and even some soups.

Wheat has been known to stimulate the appetite and even have some slight addictive qualities, so cutting it out from your diet is not a simple task.   You will need to have plenty of willpower, and remind yourself every single day that you are doing this for you, for your body, and for your own health and wellbeing.

It may not be easy, but the wheat belly diet is well worth the effort! You'll be seeing weight loss results in almost no time on this diet plan, and you are bound to feel great in other aspects of your new life, too!

Chicken Musakhan

This traditional Palestinian dish is usually made with flatbread. However, leaving it out but keeping in all the delicious flavors makes for an exciting and exotic wheat belly approved meal!

2-1/2 pounds boneless skinless chicken thighs

2 onions

1-1/2 tbsp olive oil

1 tsp cinnamon

1/4 tsp ground allspice

1/4 tsp ground cloves

1/4 tsp ground saffron

Handful of pine nuts

Salt and pepper to taste

1. Halve onions, then thinly slice.

2. Place onions, olive oil, cinnamon, allspice, cloves, and saffron in a large microwave-safe bowl.

3. Microwave on high for 3 minutes, stir, and microwave on high for an additional 2 minutes.

4. Place chicken into slow cooker.

5. Season with salt and pepper as desired.

6. Add onion mixture and stir to combine thoroughly.

7. Cover and cook on low for 7 hours.

8. In a small skillet on the stove over medium-high heat, sauté pine nuts in olive oil until browned.

9. Serve chicken topped with pine nuts.

Honey Garlic Chicken Wings

Cook up a traditional American dish of chicken wings with this tasty, fall off the bone wheat belly approved sauce!

3 pounds chicken wings

3/4 cup honey

1-1/2 tbsp minced garlic

2 tbsp olive oil

Salt and pepper to taste

1. Place chicken wings into slow cooker.

2. In a small bowl, combine honey, garlic, olive oil, salt, and pepper until liquid.   You can melt the honey on the stove if you have trouble with this step.

3. Drizzle honey sauce over wings in slow cooker.

4. Stir to combine thoroughly.

5. Cover and cook on low for 6 hours.

6. Serve.

Balsamic Chicken

Mediterranean style meals are all the rage these days. Don't get left out just because you're trying to avoid grains! This recipe will keep you enjoying Mediterranean flavors all the time!

4 skinless boneless chicken breasts

6 Italian sausages

1 onion

4 tbsp minced garlic

2 tbsp olive oil

2 tsp Italian seasoning

2 tsp garlic powder

2 tsp salt

30oz canned diced tomatoes

15oz canned tomato sauce

1 cup water

1/2 cup balsamic vinegar

1. Place chicken breasts into the bottom of the slow cooker.

2. Slice onion thinly.

3. Drizzle with 2 tbsp olive oil.

4. Place 1 tsp Italian seasoning, 1 tsp garlic powder, and 1 tsp salt on chicken.

5. Top with sausage.

6. Layer on onion and garlic.

7. Pour diced tomatoes, tomato sauce, water, and balsamic vinegar over all ingredients in the slow cooker.

8. Top with 1 tsp Italian seasoning, 1 tsp garlic powder, and 1 tsp salt.

9. Cover and cook on high for 5 hours.

10. Serve.

Cinnamon Chicken

This ultra easy few-ingredient chicken recipe can be prepared ahead of time and the raw ingredients can be frozen for quick cooking in the slow cooker any day of the week!

2 pounds chicken breasts

2 bell peppers

1 onion

2 tsp paprika

4 tbsp minced garlic

2 tsp cinnamon

1 cup chicken broth

1/4 tsp nutmeg

1. Place chicken into slow cooker.

2. Season chicken with paprika, garlic, and cinnamon.

3. Dice bell peppers and onion and place over chicken and spices in slow cooker.

4. Pour over chicken broth and sprinkle in nutmeg.

5. Stir everything.

6. Cover and cook on low for 6 hours.

7. Serve.

Stuffed Chicken

Enjoy all the delicious flavors of a stuffed chicken breast without any of the added problems of grains with this amazing recipe.

4 boneless skinless chicken breasts

1 tbsp olive oil

1/2 onion

1/2 red bell pepper

2 pepperoncini peppers

6oz spinach

2 tsp minced garlic

1/2 tsp dried oregano

Salt and pepper to taste

1 cup chicken stock

1/2 cup white wine (optional)

1/3 cup feta cheese

1. Dice onions.

2. Cut red bell pepper and pepperoncini peppers into thin strips.

3. Slice a deep pocket into each chicken breast.

4. Salt and pepper each chicken breast.

5. In a large skillet over medium heat, cook peppers and onion in olive oil for 2 minutes.

6. Add garlic and spinach and cook until spinach wilts.

7. Add oregano, stir, and remove from heat.

8. Stuff feta into chicken.

9. Spoon spinach mixture into each chicken.

10. Place stuffed chicken breasts into slow cooker.

11. Pour over chicken stock and optional white win.

12. Cover and cook on low for 8 hours.

13. Serve.

Cranberry Apple Turkey

This recipe makes an excellent, simple wheat belly Thanksgiving dinner! Serve it up with mashed potatoes, spaghetti squash, green beans, and any other veggie sides you love for the holidays.

5 pound bone-in skin-on turkey breast

3 apples

4 cups raw cranberries

Salt

1/2 cup apple cider vinegar

1/2 cup maple syrup

1. Slice apples; peel or don't peel, your choice.

2. Place turkey breast into the slow cooker.

3. Sprinkle with salt.

4. Top and surround with apples and cranberries.

5. Pour over vinegar and maple syrup.

6. Cover and cook on low for 8 hours.

7. Serve turkey topped with fruit.

Kimchi Chicken

This delightful and delicious recipe serves up yummy Asian flavors in a simple but tasty way.   Works great on its own or over cauliflower!

1 cup chicken broth

4 scallions

3 tbsp minced garlic

1 tbsp soy sauce

2 tsp palm sugar

1 tbsp sesame oil

1/4 tsp ground ginger

2 pounds boneless skinless chicken thighs

2 cups cabbage kimchi

1. Drain jarred cabbage kimchi.

2. Slice scallions and separate green and white parts.

3. Place chicken broth, minced garlic, soy sauce, palm sugar, sesame oil, and ground ginger into the slow cooker and stir to combine thoroughly.

4. Place chicken into the sauce and spoon some over the top of the chicken.

5. Cover and cook on low for 4 hours.

6. Turn heat to high.

7. Add kimchi and cook for 20 minutes.

8. Serve topped with scallions.

Mirepoix Chicken

This simple recipe can be prepared in as little as 5 minutes! Make it when you know you're going to be ultra busy but still want a delicious dinner.

1 whole chicken

Salt and pepper to taste

1 onion

2 carrots

2 stalks of celery

3 tbsp minced garlic

1 lemon

1. Juice lemon.

2. Chop onion.

3. Peel carrots.

4. Dice carrots and celery.

5. Wash chicken, then pat dry and season with salt and pepper generously.

6. Place half of the diced vegetables into the slow cooker.

7. Top with chicken.

8. Place garlic inside chicken cavity.

9. Top with remaining vegetables.

10. Pour lemon juice over chicken and vegetables, then add used lemon to slow cooker.

11. Cover and cook on low for 6 hours.

12. Serve.

Cilantro Lime Chicken

This Spanish style meal is very versatile. Use it in salads, lettuce taco wraps, or serve it with some grilled asparagus for a tasty meal!

6 pound whole chicken

1 tbsp chili powder

1 tbsp cayenne

1 tsp salt

1 tsp pepper

1 tsp cumin

3 limes

2 handfuls fresh cilantro

3 tbsp minced garlic

1 tbsp olive oil

1. Juice 2 limes.

2. Combine chili powder, cayenne, salt, pepper, and cumin to form a spice rub.

3. Rub entire chicken with spices.

4. In a blender, mix lime juice with cilantro, garlic, and olive oil.

5. Poke holes in third lime, dust with chili powder, and stuff inside chicken.

6. Marinate chicken overnight in blended lime juice marinade.

7. Place chicken and remaining marinade into slow cooker.

8. Cover and cook on low for 6 hours.

9. Serve.

So Easy Salsa Chicken

This meal takes almost no time to prepare but comes out tasting like you spent all day in the kitchen!

1-1/2 cups chickpeas

1-1/2 cups canned black beans

1-1/2 cups frozen corn

1-1/2 cup salsa

1 pound chicken thighs

1/4 cup chopped cilantro

1. Place chicken into slow cooker.

2. Drain and rinse beans and chickpeas, then add to slow cooker.

3. Add frozen corn, salsa, and chopped cilantro.

4. Stir to combine everything well.

5. Cover and cook on low for 6 hours.

6. Serve.

Chicken Gizzard Soup

Don't let the name put you off of this delicious dark meat dish! Many people are afraid of trying chicken gizzards, but they are actually a very nutritious part of the chicken that is much too often overlooked.

1 pound chicken gizzards

2 tbsp olive oil

1 cup chopped onion

2 tbsp minced garlic

Salt and pepper to taste

5 cups water

1. Quarter chicken gizzards.

2. In a large skillet on the stove over medium-high heat, cook gizzards in olive oil with onion and garlic for 10 minutes.

3. Place mixture in slow cooker.

4. Season liberally with salt and pepper.

5. Pour over water.

6. Cover and cook for 8 hours on high.

7. Serve.

Honey BBQ Ribs

This recipe is perfect for a summertime dinner or for a Game Day treat!

Olive oil

1 cup minced onion

Salt and pepper to taste

4 tbsp minced garlic

1 tsp ground cumin

1 tsp dry mustard

1 tsp dried basil

1 tsp dried oregano

1 tsp cayenne

1 cup tomato paste

1-1/2 cups chicken broth

2 tbsp apple cider vinegar

2 tbsp honey

4 pounds pork spare ribs

1. In a large skillet over medium heat, cook onions in olive oil for about 10 minutes.

2. Add garlic, cumin, mustard, basil, oregano, and cayenne and stir.

3. Add Tomato paste, chicken broth, apple cider vinegar, and honey, and whisk until mixture is smooth.

4. Bring to boil.

5. Meanwhile, season ribs with salt and pepper and place into slow cooker.

6. After mixture boils, pour over the ribs in the slow cooker.

7. Cover and cook on low for 8 hours.

8. Serve.

Lamb Roast

Just because you're dieting doesn't mean you can't indulge yourself in something fancy every now and then. Make up this delectable lamb dish and you'll be in taste heaven!

2 pounds lamb roast

16oz canned diced green chiles

15oz canned fire roasted diced tomatoes

1 bell pepper

1 tbsp cumin

1 tbsp paprika

1 tsp chili powder

1 tsp garlic powder

Salt and pepper to taste

1. Dice bell pepper finely.

2. Place lamb into slow cooker.

3. Add green chiles, tomatoes, and bell peppers.

4. Add cumin, paprika, chili powder, garlic powder, salt, and pepper.

5. Stir to combine thoroughly.

6. Cover and cook on low for 7 hours.

7. Shred and serve.

Plantain Pork

Utilize the tropical flavor of plantains in this fun recipe!

2 pound pork loin

1 onion

3 cups beef broth

1 tbsp garlic powder

1 tsp onion powder

Salt and pepper to taste

4 brown plantains

2 tbsp coconut oil

1 tsp cinnamon

1 tsp allspice

4 tbsp canned coconut milk

1. Slice onion.

2. Peel plantains and slice in half lengthwise.

3. Place pork loin into slow cooker.

4. Top with sliced onion, garlic powder, onion powder, salt, and pepper.

5. Pour over beef broth.

6. Cover and cook on low for 8 hours.

7. In a large skillet on the stove over medium heat, melt coconut oil.

8. Add sliced plantains to melted coconut oil.

9. Sprinkle plantains with cinnamon, allspice, and just a pinch of salt.

10. Cook for 5 minutes per side.

11. Place cooked plantains in a slow cooker and puree while adding coconut milk gradually.

12. Serve plantain mash topped with pork.

Jambalaya

You don't need wheat to have a delicious Jambalaya! This recipe calls for shrimp, but it can be omitted for those with shellfish allergies.

5 cups chicken stock

4 bell peppers

1 onion

1 can diced tomatoes in juice

2 tbsp minced garlic

1 pound raw de-veined large shrimp

4 oz diced precooked chicken breast

1 package spicy andouille sausage

1 head cauliflower

2 cups okra

3 tbsp cajun seasoning

1/4 cup hot sauce

1. Place peppers, onions, garlic, chicken, cajun seasoning, and hot sauce in a slow cooker.

2. Top with chicken stock and stir to combine thoroughly.

3. Cover and cook on low for 5 and a half hours.

4. Add sliced andouille sausages; cover and cook for 10 minutes on low.

5. Pulse cauliflower in a food processor or blender until it resembles rice.

6. Add cauliflower "rice" and raw shrimp to slow cooker.

7. Cover and cook for 20 minutes on low.

8. Serve.

Carnitas

Enjoy this spicy and tasty pork dish that is sweeping the nation!

4 pound pork loin roast

1 tsp garlic powder

1 tsp chili powder

1 tsp ground cumin

1 tsp salt

2 oranges

1 lime

2 cups chicken stock

2 tbsp tomato paste

1 tbsp adobo sauce

3 tbsp minced garlic

Olive oil

1. Slice roast into 2 inch thick strips.

2. In a large bowl, combine garlic powder, chili powder, ground cumin, and salt.

3. Coat pork roast strips evenly in spices.

4. In a large skillet over medium-high heat, sear pork loin strips in olive oil.

5. Place seared pork in slow cooker.

6. In the same skillet, deglaze with tomato paste, chicken stock, adobo sauce, and garlic.

7. Let broth simmer for 5 minutes.

8. Juice oranges and lime and pour juice over pork in slow cooker.

9. Pour simmered broth over pork in slow cooker.

10. Cover and cook on low for 5 hours.

11. Shred and serve.

Apple Pork

This ultra traditional pork recipe will be everyone's favorite in no time flat.

4 apples

2 pound pork tenderloin

Nutmeg to taste

2 tbsp honey

1. Core and slice apples; peel or do not peel, your choice.

2. Layer apples into the bottom of the slow cooker and sprinkle with nutmeg.

3. Slit pork tenderloin and place atop apples in slow cooker.

4. Place an apple slice in each slit in the pork tenderloin.

5. Sprinkle again with nutmeg and top with any remaining apples.

6. Cover and cook on low for 8 hours.

7. Serve.

Hawaiian Pork

Serve with a side of mashed sweet potato for an excellent taste of Hawaii!

4 pounds pork shoulder

1 can crushed pineapple

1/2 tsp dried ginger

1. Place pork into slow cooker.

2. Top with pineapple and liquid form can.

3. Sprinkle ginger on top and stir to combine.

4. Cover and cook on low for 8 hours.

5. Shred pork and serve.

Spiced Pork Shoulder

This recipe is a traditional Mexican favorite that creates a very tender pulled pork.

1 onion

15oz canned fire roasted diced tomatoes

2 tbsp paprika

1 tsp ground cumin

1 tsp black pepper

1 tsp salt

1 tsp nutmeg

5 pound pork shoulder

1 orange

1/4 cup apple cider vinegar

1. Juice orange.

2. In a small bowl, combine paprika, cumin, black pepper, salt, and nutmeg. Ad a small amount of water to create a spice paste.

3. Slice onion and place in a large skillet over medium heat.

4. Cook for 5 minutes, then pour in canned tomatoes with juice.

5. Cook for 5 minutes more.

6. Slice 2 inch strips from pork shoulder.

7. Pour orange juice into slow cooker and mix with apple cider vinegar.

8. Add in spice paste and stir until thoroughly dissolved.

9. Place pork into liquid.

10. Top with tomatoes and onions.

11. Cover and cook on low for 8 hours.

12. Serve, optionally with some fried eggs.

Spare Ribs

Serve these Asian style ribs over simple microwave steamed vegetables for a tasty dinner the whole family will love!

4 pounds pork ribs

4 cups white vinegar

2 cups water

1 tsp salt

2 tbsp apple cider vinegar

3 tbsp soy sauce

Salt and pepper to taste

Garlic powder to taste

1. Soak ribs in vinegar with a tsp of sea salt overnight.

2. Drain thoroughly.

3. Season ribs generously all over with salt, pepper, and garlic powder.

4. Place ribs upright in slow cooker.

5. Add apple cider vinegar and soy sauce to slow cooker.

6. Cover and cook on high for 5 hours.

7. Serve.

Lamb Pumpkin Curry

This recipe is full of unique and delightful flavors, and it's so packed with protein you're sure to feel amazing after you devour it!

4 lamb shanks

1 pound pumpkin puree

1 onion

2 tbsp minced garlic

1 cup coconut milk

4 cups water

1 tbsp ground ginger

1 tbsp paprika

1 tbsp cumin

1 tbsp turmeric

1 tsp chili powder

1 tsp cinnamon

Salt and pepper to taste

1. Dice onion.
2. Place onion into slow cooker with garlic, ginger, paprika, cumin, turmeric, chili powder, cinnamon, salt and pepper, coconut milk, and water.

3. Stir to combine everything thoroughly.

4. Add lamb shanks and stir to coat.

5. Cover and cook on low for 2 hours.

6. Add pumpkin puree and stir to mix in thoroughly.

7. Cover and cook on low for 6 hours.

8. Pull meat from bones if necessary.

9. Serve.

Pot Roast

This ultra traditional crock pot dish is perfect for a weekly Friday night dinner.

4 pound beef chuck roast

1 tbsp olive oil

1 cup red wine

2 tbsp minced garlic

1 tbsp dried thyme

1 carrot

2 stalks celery

1 onion

1 head cauliflower

Salt and pepper to taste

1. Peel carrot and cut into chunks.

2. Cut celery and onion into chunks as well.

3. Cut florets from cauliflower.

4. Season beef with salt and pepper.

5. In a large skillet over medium high heat on the stove, sear beef quickly in olive oil.

6. Pour red wine into hot skillet and boil quickly.   Scrape the bottom of the pan into the wine.

7. Pour mixture over beef.

8. Place garlic and thyme into slow cooker.

9. Add carrot, celery, and onion to slow cooker.

10. Stir to combine everything thoroughly.

11. Cover and cook on low for 8 hours.

12. Add cauliflower.

13. Cover and cook on low for 20 minutes.

14. Serve.

Portobello Mushroom Sandwiches

These delicious sandwiches make a quick and easy meal that is as fun to make as it is to eat!

2-1/2 pounds beef chuck roast

1 tsp dried basil

1 tsp dried oregano

1 tsp dried rosemary

1 tsp garlic powder

1 tsp onion powder

Salt and pepper to taste

1/2 cup water

1 tbsp red wine vinegar

2 tbsp dijon mustard

6 large portobello mushroom caps

1. Combine basil, oregano, rosemary, garlic powder, onion powder, salt, and pepper in a small bowl to form a rub.

2. Rub meat with spices.

3. In a large skillet over medium-high heat, sear spiced meat for 5 minutes per side.

4. Place meat into slow cooker and cover with red wine vinegar and water.

5. Cover and cook on low for 8 hours.

6. Shred meat and remove.

7. Add dijon mustard to liquid in slow cooker and stir to combine.

8. Add shredded beef back to slow cooker to coat with dijon sauce.

9. Spoon onto portobollo mushrooms as buns.

10. Serve.

Coffee Beef

This yummy and savory beef is great on its own or in lettuce tacos.

1 beef roast

2 tbsp minced garlic

2 tsp cocoa powder

3 tbsp ancho chile powder

1 tsp dried oregano

1 tsp cinnamon

1 tsp cumin

1 tsp chipotle powder

1 tsp salt

3/4 cup strong brewed coffee

1 tbsp balsamic vinegar

1. In a large bowl, combine garlic, cocoa powder, chile powder, dried oregano, cinnamon, cumin, chipotle powder, and salt. Add a bit of water to create a spice paste.

2. Rub beef with spice paste.

3. Place beef roast into slow cooker.

4. Stir together coffee and vinegar; pour over beef roast in slow cooker.

5. Cover and cook on low for 8 hours.

6. Serve.

Beef Tongue

Beef tongue may be an acquired taste, but this recipe will definitely prove how great it can be!

1 beef tongue

1 onion

3 tbsp minced garlic

Salt and pepper to taste

Water to cover tongue in slow cooker

1. Slice onion.

2. Wash beef tongue and pat dry.

3. Place onion and garlic in bottom of slow cooker.

4. Lay tongue on top and season with salt and pepper.

5. Cover with water.

6. Cover and cook on low for 8 hours.

7. Remove skin from tongue and discard.

8. Shred and serve.

Spaghetti and Meatballs

No wheat belly crock pot cookbook would be complete without some perfectly prepared meatballs! Serve with spaghetti squash noodles for an excellent meal.

1 pound ground Italian sausage

14oz can tomato sauce

2 tbsp hot pepper relish

3 tbsp minced garlic

2 tbsp olive oil

Italian seasoning to taste

1. Place tomato sauce, olive oil, garlic, pepper relish, and Italian seasoning in slow cooker and stir to combine thoroughly.

2. Roll ground sausage into balls and place in slow cooker.

3. Cover and cook on high for 3 hours.

4. Serve.

Corned Beef

It doesn't have to be St. Patrick's Day for you to enjoy scrumptious corned beef with a side of hearty cabbage.

6 carrots

2 onions

1 cabbage

3 pound corned beef brisket with seasoning packet

3 cups water

1. Chop carrots and onions.

2. Cut cabbage into wedges.

3. Place carrots, onions, and cabbage into slow cooker.

4. Top with corned beef brisket.

5. Sprinkle seasoning packet over ingredients ins low cooker.

6. Pour water over everything.

7. Cover and cook on low for 8 hours.

8. Slice and serve.

Korean BBQ Ribs

This yummy recipe will supply you with plenty of light and spicy Asian flavors.   Goes great over a salad, too!

3 pounds beef short ribs

1 onion

2 tbsp minced garlic

1 tsp dried ginger

1/2 cup soy sauce

1/2 cup rice wine vinegar

1/4 cup honey

1 tsp red pepper flakes

2 tsp sesame oil

1/2 cup chopped scallions

Salt and pepper to taste

1. Thinly slice onion.

2. In slow cooker, combine soy sauce with rice wine vinegar, sesame oil and honey and mix well.

3. Add onion, garlic, ginger, and red pepper flakes, and stir.

4. Season ribs with salt and pepper generously.

5. Place ribs into slow cooker.

6. Cover and cook on high for 8 hours.

7. Shred beef from bones and stir to combine.

8. Serve topped with scallions.

Stroganoff

Serve over wheat-free noodles, spaghetti squash, cauliflower rice, or salad!   The possibilities are endless!

2 pounds ground beef

2 onions

2 pounds crimini mushrooms

2 tbsp minced garlic

2 tbsp dijon mustard

2 tbsp worcestershire sauce

3/4 cup coconut milk

3/4 cup beef stock

3/4 cup plain Greek yogurt

Salt and pepper to taste

1. Dice onions and slice mushrooms.

2. In a large skillet over medium high heat on the stove, brown ground beef. Season with salt and pepper to taste.

3. Stir dijon mustard and worcestershire sauce into the bottom of the slow cooker.

4. Add mushrooms, onions, and garlic to slow cooker.

5. Add browned ground beef to slow cooker.

6. Add coconut milk and beef stock, and stir to combine everything thoroughly.

7. Cover and cook on low for 8 hours.

8. Let sit for 15 minutes uncovered and way from heat.

9. When cool, stir in yogurt.

10. Serve.

Swiss Steak

This hearty meal is perfect for a cold, rainy day.

2 pounds beef round

1/4 cup arrowroot starch

2 tsp mustard powder

1 tsp dried sage

1 tsp dried thyme

2 tsp salt

1 tsp black pepper

4 carrots

4 stalks celery

1 onion

3 tbsp minced garlic

28oz can crushed tomatoes

3 tbsp worcestershire sauce

2 tbsp olive oil

1. Slice onion.

2. Peel carrots.

3. Cut beef into large cubes.

4. Combine arrowroot starch with mustard, sage, thyme, salt, and pepper.

5. Cut carrots and celery into three inch pieces.

6. Coat beef with spices.

7. In a large skillet over medium-high heat on the stove, sear spiced beef cubes in olive oil.

8. Place browned meat into slow cooker.

9. Add carrots, celery, onions, and garlic to skillet and fry for 3 minutes.

10. Place vegetable mixture in slow cooker.

11. Add tomatoes and sauce to skillet to deglaze.

12. Pour sauce over everything in slow cooker.

13. Cover and cook on low for 9 hours.

14. Serve.

Roast 'n Squash

For all the flavors of fall, make this easy chuck roast!

5 pound beef chuck roast

3 pound butternut squash

8oz can diced fire roasted tomatoes

2 tbsp minced garlic

1 tsp cumin

1 tsp paprika

2 tsp onion powder

Salt and pepper to taste

1. Halve squash and remove seeds.

2. Poke holes into chuck roast and tuck minced garlic into the holes.

3. In a small bowl, combine cumin, paprika, onion powder, salt, and pepper to form a spice rub.

4. Rub beef with spices.

5. Place beef into slow cooker.

6. Cover with canned tomatoes.

7. Place squash into slow cooker with the skin down.

8. Cover and cook on low for 6 hours.

9. Scoop out squash flesh and mash it.

10. Shred beef.

11. Serve.

Monday
>Breakfast - Cantaloupe and Blueberries
>Lunch - Salad with Oil and Vinegar
>Dinner - Honey Garlic Chicken Wings

Shopping List
cantaloupe
blueberries
salad greens
olive oil
vinegar
3 pounds chicken wings
honey
minced garlic

Tuesday
>Breakfast - Cantaloupe and Blueberries
>Lunch - leftover Honey Garlic Chicken Wings
>Dinner - Plantain Pork

Shopping List
cantaloupe
blueberries
2 pound pork loin
1 onion
beef broth
garlic powder
onion powder
4 brown plantains
coconut oil
cinnamon
allspice
canned coconut milk

Wednesday
>Breakfast - Cantaloupe and Blueberries
>Lunch - leftover Plantain Pork
>Dinner - Lamb Pumpkin Curry

Shopping List
cantaloupe
blueberries
4 lamb shanks
1 pound pumpkin puree
1 onion
minced garlic

coconut milk
ground ginger
paprika
cumin
turmeric
chili powder
cinnamon

Thursday

Breakfast - Cantaloupe and Blueberries
Lunch - leftover Lamb Pumpkin Curry
Dinner - Cinnamon Chicken

Shopping List
cantaloupe
blueberries
2 pounds chicken breasts
2 bell peppers
1 onion
paprika
minced garlic
cinnamon
chicken broth
nutmeg

Friday

Breakfast - Cantaloupe and Blueberries
Lunch - leftover Cinnamon Chicken
Dinner - Apple Pork

Shopping List
cantaloupe
blueberries
4 apples
2 pound pork tenderloin
nutmeg
honey

Saturday

Breakfast - Bacon and Eggs
Lunch - leftover Apple Pork
Dinner - Lamb Roast

Shopping List
bacon
eggs
2 pounds lamb roast
16oz canned diced green chiles
15oz canned fire roasted diced tomatoes
1 bell pepper

cumin
paprika
chili powder
garlic powder

Sunday
Breakfast - Bacon and Eggs
Lunch - leftover Lamb Roast
Dinner - Cranberry Apple Turkey
Shopping List
bacon
eggs
5 pound turkey breast
3 apples
4 cups raw cranberries
apple cider vinegar
maple syrup

Conclusion

Thank you again for downloading this book!

I hope this book was able to help you to learn how to create several new and exciting wheat belly recipes using your slow cooker.

The next step is to start cooking!

Made in the USA
Lexington, KY
18 January 2017